The Poetry Playlist

ONE STEP AT A TIME

AURORA BURKHART

ISBN: 979-8-9884426-8-4
Printed in the U.S.A.

Publisher Information:
Missfit Press
Colorado Springs, CO
www.missfitpress.com

First Edition
March 2025

Acknowledgements

"This book of poems is so special because not only do they vary from what emotions they evoke and trigger, but they are beautifully paired with a song that heightens those emotions and really brings to the whole experience. You will find some that resonate with you and bring tears to your eyes and then, a few pages later, you will feel strong and empowered."

—Taylor Carver

"Stories of struggles, strength, and a rise to greatness that everyone can relate to. The power and openness Aurora takes us through while reading her poems opens your minds and hearts to the beauty and growth. It grants the reader the opportunity to reflect on difficult times and the hope that carries our soul through them. Beautiful, inspiring and raw. A must-have to keep nearby when your guiding light starts to fade."

—Emily Bonderer

"One Step at a Time is a captivating collection of poems that dives deep into the human experience. Each verse is rich with thought and emotion, offering raw, relatable reflections that at times feel like the lyrics of a great emo song—achingly beautiful, yet profoundly inspiring. These poems don't just

resonate; they challenge you to confront life's struggles and remind you that your path is always yours to choose. It's a must-read for anyone seeking connection, solace, or a fresh perspective on their own journey."

—Jessica O'Malley

"A MUST READ! One Step at a Time takes you on an emotional journey. It is an absolute masterpiece capturing aspects of pain and self-healing using an innovative approach—each poem carefully paired with a song to paint a raw and vivid picture. This beautifully curated piece uses fierce figurative language, creating a moving experience and inspiring the reader to find peace…one step at a time."

–Jillian Bothwell

"This collection of written works goes straight to the heart. Each one is written with palpable emotion. A. Burkhart captures emotions that most every adolescent comes face-to-face with. There is so much beauty and pain in the words she so carefully weaves together. Truly a wonderful celebration of growth and overcoming."

—Karly Delatorre

"One Step at a Time is unlike anything I've ever read. The beautiful pairing of the written word to a song captures the senses in a raw, spellbinding experience. The reader feels their

heart break, yet come back together anew. A true literary masterpiece for your mind, body, and soul!"
  –Emily Hardesty

"Beautiful thought-out poems that personify the depths in which darkness can seep within ourselves, wreaking havoc on our minds, bodies, and souls. Aurora brings to light the imperfections of the monotony of life, the everyday monologue that too many of us have but are too afraid to voice. Be not afraid to dive in and explore these thoughts of despair and hopelessness, for everything can be overcome when you have the courage to persevere and take one step at a time.
  –Katie Pekich

To the fighters—
May you find a peaceful place to lay down your armor while you rest.
To the dreamers—
May you remind the stars that you are one in the same.
To the misfits—
May you never abandon your cause.
To the lovers—
May you always have an abundance of trust.
To the lost—
May you wander with serenity.

To you, from me.

Playlist

Disclaimer

The content of this book may be sensitive to some audiences. It includes themes of extreme emotion that may trigger some readers. Reader discretion is advised.

Download the Playlist

Spotify

To the Rebellious Ones

Night We Met
Lord Huron

*T*o the rebellious ones
To the difficult ones–
You give the others a fighting chance.
You change it from a dialogue to a conversation.
You change it from fact to opinion.
You change it from required to elective.
You change it from immunity to accountability.

*T*his apology is long overdue.
Dear me,
I'm so sorry.
I'm sorry–
For not only did I let others undervalue us, but I did as well.
I'm sorry–
For being our harshest critic.
I'm sorry–
For trying to convince us that we were unworthy of our dreams.
I'm sorry–
For not leaving sooner, because I felt I couldn't lead us.
I'm sorry–
For taking so long to heal our wounds, because I was afraid to let go of the pain.

2

I don't want to be haunted.
Haunted by the ghost of the version of me
that will never exist.
All because I chose to merely survive
And to not live.
I'd rather go to my grave earlier
Than be haunted while I live.

T hey feed you poison–
then ask why you are struggling to
survive.
With a flick of their tongue, their words cut deep.
They then question how you became a master of
Smith.
They keep you locked up in the dark
Then ask why you are haunted.
They give you nothing–
Then ask why you took everything when you
walked away.

T hey say my voice is too loud–
They are just used to whispering.
They say I dream too big–
They haven't dreamt in a long time.
They say I am selfish–
They never choose themselves.

They say I have no friends–
They are more lonely than I am.
They say I should be like them–
I say we should be ourselves; whatever that may be.

I feel disconnected.
No one notices how my smile doesn't
reach my eyes,
How my silence comes from lack of relation, not
shyness.
I long for a connection, but it seems to be out of
range.
I'd rather be disconnected from everyone than
connected to anyone.

I have to succeed.
I've always heard the call to this destiny.
Because it's not just mine,
it's theirs too.
I am picking up where they left off.
I am guided by the ones who came before me.
I will succeed because they sacrificed for me to
reach the starting line.
I was chosen to finish it.

Dear Me,

I'm so sorry_____

_____

_____

_____

_____

_____

_____

_____

_____

_____

_____

_____

_____

_____

Share your thoughts with the_poetry_playlist

You Did It

Baby, I'm a Gangster Too
Briarr

*Y*ou did it.
You became the monster you hoped
would save you.
You know that no one was meant to save you,
since you were created for this.
The monster that can't be destroyed and will protect
others ruthlessly–
Go show them what good and evil can do.

*Y*ou don't like me?
You don't like that I won't tolerate your
disrespect?
You don't like my retribution?
You haven't seen anything yet, sweetheart.
Buckle up, because you're about to hate me.

*R*emember who you are.
When they threw you into the fire,
you were reborn a Phoenix, rising from
the ashes.
When you were hurled into the arena,
You emerged victorious and undefeated.
When they exiled you,
An army forged to avenge you.
They intended to break you with all they did.
Rather, they turned you into a formidable opponent.

*G*o ahead, my love,
take it all off.
Take off your armor.
Disarm yourself.
Let your guard down.
Let your mind go silent.
When you're with me, you are safe.
I'll stand watch over you.
I protect what's mine.

*Y*ou've never had my love before, so let me
elaborate–
I will protect you.
I will protect your heart, your mind, and your name.
I will be loyal to only you.
Others will never feel comfortable speaking ill of
you in my presence.
My eyes and heart are devoted to you.
I will support you.
I will make your dreams my dreams.
I will do everything and anything to help you reach
your full potential.
I will always keep you company.
On your darkest days, I will sit with you.
On your best days, I will be celebrating with you.
On your weakest days, I will lend you my strength.

9

Oh, you don't like it, do you?
Let me bring you to life
only to control your movements.
Let me starve you of humility
Then expect undying loyalty in return.
Let me appreciate your beauty
Then shame you for when others admire.
Let me take away your gentleness
Then be shocked when I am met with indifference.
Let me take everything away I love
Then become well acquainted with hate.

How do you define loyalty? _____

_____

_____

_____

_____

_____

_____

_____

_____

_____

_____

_____

_____

Share your thoughts with the_poetry_playlist

I'm Sorry

Elastic Heart
Sia

I'm sorry.
I'm sorry you had to find out how strong
you are.
I'm sorry you have to grieve what happened
and grieve a part of yourself that died as well.
I'm sorry you feel like a bystander in your own life.
I'm sorry you yearn for another life
and want this one to end.
I'm sorry the darkness made your light brighter.

*Y*ou want to know why people root for the
underdog?
Because the underdog has no advantages.
Ironically, that became their biggest advantage.
Because they have a mentality we all wish we had
without having gone through half of what they did.
They are prepared to lose friends and family
If it means they gain peace.
They have the most powerful faith we have ever
seen.
They believed in themselves, when no one else did.
They have the kindest souls, even though they went
through hell.
We all wish we could be the underdog—
But we are too afraid.

*Y*ou might think you're immune, but no one
is.
We all have it.
A blind spot.
Even the Greats have one.
But are you willing to leave them in the rearview
mirror—
Before they wreck you?

I don't fit in.
And I hope I never do.
You say you don't dream.
I dream so often that I have created an infinite
number of universes.
I don't just love—
I love with every thought, breath, and touch.
If I choose to be in your life,
You will never be alone again.
Even if you need to sit in the dark and heal,
I'll sit with you.
I have high expectations for my life.
I don't think I am better—
I just know what I am capable of.
When it's my time to go
I want to say it was well spent;
I was an active participant;
I used every gift I was given;

I gave more than I took.

*T*hey tell you it's all in your head.
They tell you that you have no reason to
be angry.
But you know you deserve better than how they
treated you.
They tell you that you have unrealistic
expectations—
You asked for the bare minimum.
They say you can never be happy—
You gave everything and were given nothing in
return.
They can no longer control you—
You now know that you are the creator of your own
destiny.

*W*hen they keep coming for your light,
do not dim it—
For it means you are on the right path.
They don't want you to bring things to light.
They live in the darkness, lurking in the shadows,
snuffing out the other's light.
Or intimidate them into taking unsteady breaths
that only force them to blow out their own light.
Stand tall.

Remain unwavering.
Steady your breath.
And stare the darkness down,
for your light will force them out of your path.

*B*ecause of you I was burned from the torch
you passed on to me.
Because of you I was burned to save the
others.
Because of you I flinch when I feel any warmth.
Because of you I would rather sit in the cold
darkness.
Because of you I mistook your flame for survival.

*I don't fit in. I am the underdog.*_____

_____

_____

_____

_____

_____

_____

_____

_____

_____

_____

_____

_____

_____

Share your thoughts with the_poetry_playlist

I Wish I Could Go Back

Dynasty
MIIA

I wish I could go back—
Go back in time.
I would run up to you and hug you.
As I held on, I would tell you—
It's ok.
You did your best.
You didn't know what it was like to stand in the
sun.
I turned out ok.
I crawled through the darkness and found my way
out.
I no longer hold resentment.
I found the light.
Now I am filled with remorse that you never did.
It's ok.
I'm ok.
You did your best,
and I took care of the rest.

I understand it now.
You were trying to save me;
Protecting me the best way you knew how.
You wanted me to lay down and lie still,
So no one and nothing could harm me.
But I ended up laying in my grave,
Looking up still being able to see life pass me by.

*R*emember this—
There are people who bought tickets to
your show hoping you fail—
Yet they will always remain in the stands.
There are people echoing your sentiments—
Yet they are silent when your name is being
attacked.
There are people whose smiles are not from their
fondness of you—
Yet, from the anticipation of their schemes, plotted
against you.
They support you—
By supporting allegiance to your enemies.

*I*t's a lie.
You get to choose your village.
It will consist of people who say
"I support you."
"I may or may not agree with your choice,
but this is your path."
"I'm here to support you however you need."
"How can I help?"
Your village will never shame you.
Your village wants to provide for you.
They will never ask for payment in return.
Your village wants you to thrive, not merely
survive.

*I*t never goes away.
It ebbs and flows.
It's a daily battle.
It's learning to grow around the grief,
For it will never leave you.
Grief is not your enemy—
It is an acquaintance of longing.
You long to hold them again,
But know you can't.
Refusing to forget them.
Grief sits with you.
Grief bridges the friendship between longing and
forgetting.

*If I could go back in time, I would tell myself*____

_____

_____

_____

_____

_____

_____

_____

_____

_____

_____

_____

_____

_____

Share your thoughts with the_poetry_playlist

You Did Nothing Wrong, My Love

Luminary
Joel Sunny

You did nothing wrong, my love.
You finally stood in your power.
They never wanted you to discover your true self,
For they knew you would become invincible and uncontrollable.
Stand tall,
Keep your chin up,
And unapologetically be yourself.
You have arrived.

Once you make the choice, you can't come back.
The reality you once knew will be exposed.
You will no longer have the viewpoint of the audience.
The main priority is to be entertained and distracted.
Once you go behind the curtain,
You will see the strings.
You meet the puppeteer.
You see how much effort they put into holding and directing the audience's attention.
It is so obvious now.
But you see the glazed over eyes of the audience—
They laugh and cry on cue.

Their emotions, thoughts, and desires are all controlled.
You understand it now—
And there's no going back.

I've always dreamed differently from the rest.
My nightmares inspire me.
How? You may ask—
Because my nightmares consist of me living someone else's dream rather than my own.
My favorite dreams are those in which I wake up crying and struggling to catch my breath.
My greatest dreams—
They awaken me.

*I*t's happening.
You need to be patient—
You are almost there.
I know you're exhausted,
But you must keep going.
Allow me to tell you something—
Did you know that a bamboo plant takes five years to break through the ground?
For five years, the plant grows
And becomes stronger by the day.

Then one day, it sprouts
And grows at an astonishing rate.
Those five years go unnoticed, since they did not
witness the effort and growth.
They only celebrate the result.
They only celebrate their definition of success.
The bamboo plant should be respected for its
perseverance and patience.
Growing alone in the dark,
When no one believed in you
Except for yourself,
Is the true definition of success.
Keep going—
I believe in you.

*T*o the ones who feel too much—
You don't feel too much.
You feel for yourself and you feel what
they refuse to.
You mourn for them,
For they choose not to live.
They believe they can walk this earth,
Picking and choosing when to be alive,
For they are more dead than alive.
You, my love,
Carry the most life.

*T*he difference between the Hero and the
Villain—
One wants to shield everyone from
experiencing the pain they suffered,
The other wants everyone to join them in their pain
And suffer more than they did.
One diminished the pain,
The other magnified the pain.
Who will you become?

*How can you stand in your power?*_____

_____

_____

_____

_____

_____

_____

_____

_____

_____

_____

_____

_____

_____

_____

Share your thoughts with the_poetry_playlist

People Treat You How You Allow Them To

Lion
Saint Mesa

*P*eople treat you how you allow them to.
It's a reflection of the standards you hold
for yourself.
Trust me, they know what they are doing.
So, don't tolerate less than you deserve.
Burn bridges as needed—
You know how to swim.

*M*y love, you need to realize this.
It's not that they don't love you—
It's that they can only love you to the
capacity that they love themselves.
It's not that they can't be honest—
It's that they can't even be honest with themselves,
let alone you.
It's not that they don't have faith in you—
It's that they don't even believe in themselves.
It's not that they don't support you—
It's that they, themselves, can't even imagine being
as ambitious as you are.
It's not that they think you are cocky—
It's that they don't have a fraction of your
confidence.
It has everything to do with them,
And nothing to do with you.

*Y*ou think it is scary that people are judging you?
It's haunting to get to the end of your life,
And realize you lived a life for others.
Do you think it's scary to tell someone you love them?
It's haunting to let the love of your life go by,
because you were a coward.
You think it's scary to take a risk?
It's haunting to arrive at your deathbed with regrets.
Do you want to be scared or haunted?

*Y*ou want to know the reason why they talk about you to others?
Because they can no longer control you,
So they try to control the narrative.
Let them.
If people are willing to blindly accept their point of view,
Let them.
Surround yourself with people who wouldn't tolerate your name being spoken in an ill manner around them.

You think you understand my pain?
It took me too long to understand that the
pain I was experiencing wasn't my own.
It was theirs.
They hated me for the things they hated about
themselves.
Their wounds caused me to bleed.
They broke pieces of me to reflect their own.
Everything I suffered was not my own.
I was reborn when I learned they were trying to
bring back a ghost rather than giving me life.

I've always known I was different from the
rest.
While others were shocked,
I was unfazed.
They went mad in the darkness—
It's where I found my strength.
When they needed others to save them,
I was becoming my own savior.
You say it's unfair.
I say it's many people's reality, including mine.
You want sunshine and rainbows—
I want the most powerful storms,
Because that is where power lies.
You run from your monsters—
I tamed mine.

*You are the Lion. How do you rule your jungle?*___

_____

_____

_____

_____

_____

_____

_____

_____

_____

_____

_____

Share your thoughts with the_poetry_playlist

You Think I'm Not a Threat

Bow
Reyn Hartley

You think I'm not a threat—
You mistake my silence for submission.
You mistake my lack of confrontation for fear.
Oh honey,
Why is it that you now find yourself at a loss for words?
You feel insanity creep into your mind like an inevitable storm.
I was never unprepared or afraid—
I was patiently waiting for the perfect opportunity to strike at your greatest weakness.
You think attacking at the surface will do the most damage.
I know annihilating from within is the most lethal.

Go ahead, light the match,
And watch me burn brighter.
Go ahead, send everyone you have after me—
Watch me obliterate your sense of security.
Go ahead, tell me your pretty little lies—
Watch me cast spells with mine.
Go ahead.

*N*o, I don't think I'm better than everyone
else.
Unlike the rest,
I know my worth.
If you think my worth is too high for you,
Then leave.
I don't negotiate.

I am drawn to power,
But not for the reasons you assume.
I am drawn to power because in order to
possess, own, and maintain it,
You have to overcome obstacles you never
imagined you'd confront—
Let alone come out victorious.
Power comes from discipline,
And the ability to bend forces to your will.
Power comes from understanding—
When to be compassionate,
And when to be ruthless.

What ways can you keep your power? _____

_____

_____

_____

_____

_____

_____

_____

_____

_____

_____

_____

_____

_____

Share your thoughts with the_poetry_playlist

They are
Unable to
Comprehend

Mount Everest
Labrinth

*T*hey are unable to comprehend
How different your life is from theirs.
They go searching for the pack—
The pack seeks you out.
They need someone to tell them what to do—
You follow your own compass.
They need a pack to survive—
The pack needs you to survive.
They cower when someone challenges them—
You must restrain your response,
To reduce the damage you will inflict.
You are built different.

*B*e the bigger person?
No.
If I need to constantly be the bigger person,
Then I am around small people.
Respectfully, you have no place in my life.
Disrespectfully, open that small mind of yours and increase your self-awareness.
The world shouldn't coddle you for what you lack.
Walk away with your head held high.

*W*hy do you do that to yourself?
You value the opinions of people who
don't value themselves.
You have to realize this.
They are not telling you what your capabilities
are—
They are projecting their capabilities onto you.
They don't believe in themselves—
They believe in playing it safe.
So, before you put too much stock in their opinions,
Ask yourself this—
Do you want the same results as them?
Because if you do, you will have the same
problems.

I choose peace.
I choose peace over being accepted.
I choose peace over fitting in.
I choose peace over being with the wrong person.
I choose peace over fitting into their boxes.
I choose peace over being "normal".
I choose peace over being conditionally supported.
Peace is living my life the way I want to—
For when I am in my last seconds,
It will be filled with peace and not regret.

*Y*ou are not privileged to know my next
move.
It's not because I am afraid of you—
It's because you are not on my team.
People on my team
Will block others in my path
And assist as needed.
You only want to see me lose.

I'm delusional?
Let me tell you what is truly delusional—
Believing you have limits that were set by
others;
That it's a mistake to start over;
You should go with the masses and never stand
alone;
That vulnerability is weakness;
When others laugh at you, it must mean you are the
crazy one;
That your energy is not pure magic;
That "no" is actually redirection and not rejection.
Once you accept this,
There is nothing that you cannot bring to fruition.

*What is the difference between pack mentality and alpha mentality?*_____

_____

_____

_____

_____

_____

_____

_____

_____

_____

_____

_____

_____

Share your thoughts with the_poetry_playlist

I'd Rather Feel My Heart Shatter

Royalty
Egzod, Maestro Chives, Neoni

I'd rather feel my heart shatter than
nothing.
I would rather choose to be broken and
alone,
Than surrounded by people who pretend to love me,
But pray for my demise.
I'd rather live in solitude
Than live a life with others whose heads are buried
in the sand.
I'd rather be on the brink of death, time and time
again
Than to arrive at death's doorstep never having
lived.
I'd rather have everyone mock me
Than be an obedient, mindless soldier.
I choose to live then die,
Instead of dying,
Wishing I had lived.

*T*hink of yourself as a piece of art.
Some will look at you and acknowledge
the matter of fact—you are art.
But there is only recognition and not a true
understanding.
There is no longing in their gaze.
There is no feeling of old souls who found one
another once again.

Surround yourself with people who appreciate the colors and vibrancy you bring.
How you can connect with people of all walks of life—
There will be no need to water yourself down—
If they do not appreciate you, let them walk away.
They do not understand the worth you bring;
The peace you bring.
For there are others—
Others that are thankful to be able to hear your unspoken message;
Others that are grateful to have been able to just lay eyes upon you;
Others that want to share the value you bring to the world.
They don't need your message to be written out for them to explain what they are experiencing.
Energy doesn't need to be transcribed.

*L*et them.
Let them call you insane.
Let them laugh at you.
Let them whisper as soon as you pass.
For you are not like them—
You see possibilities they couldn't even dream of.
You are not meant to be in their world.
So continue to see the music.

Continue to dream in colors that don't exist.
Continue to solve problems that others don't see—
And let them.

*M*ost will never understand the true meaning of success.
It's not having unlimited money in the bank.
It's not having the 2.5 kids with a picket fence.
It's creating your own peace—
That is something no one can take from you.
Everything can be going up in flames,
While everyone you trusted is abandoning you,
Yet, you can remain calm,
Because you trust yourself enough to know you will survive.
Nothing and no one can destroy what you have built,
Because building peace is building unwavering trust with yourself.

*L*ife isn't fair, this I know.
I live in the trenches.
Yet, you are a visitor—
You tell me to hold on,
That it will end soon.

It's easy to say when you aren't shoulder to
shoulder with insanity and death—
Both are becoming more convincing by the day.
The irony of being in the trenches
Is hiding in the ground accompanied with the graves
of others,
Only in hopes that it will keep you safe enough to
live another day.
But you tell me to hold on,
And it will end soon.

S elect your thoughts and you select your
friends.
Select your thoughts and you select your
career.
Select your thoughts and you select your partner.
Select your thoughts and you select your problems.
Select your thoughts and you select your life.
Select your thoughts and watch them materialize.

Let them. _____

_____

_____

_____

_____

_____

_____

_____

_____

_____

_____

_____

_____

_____

_____

Share your thoughts with the_poetry_playlist

I Wish I Could, but I Can't Do It

Everything Works Out In the End
Luke Willies

I wish I could, but I can't do it.
I can't do it for you.
I can show you the path—
But I can't carry you.
I can offer you a spark—
But you must transform it into a steady flame.
I can give you the tools—
But you have to build it yourself.
I promise I won't leave you.
But I can't do it.
The only way you can be saved
Is by saving yourself.

*P*ut it down.
You weren't supposed to carry it—
This wasn't your burden to bear.
They didn't heal,
So they passed it down to you.
Let it go.
And let it end with you.

I've grown to believe that the best people
are paradoxical.
The ones with the gentlest hearts
Have experienced the most anguish.
The silent ones

Are the ones you should seek guidance from.
The recluses
Know true peace and acceptance.
The people with the most scars
Have the most beautiful souls.

"You don't care."
She used to.
The old version of me did.
She used to give, even when she had nothing left.
She used to forgive, even when they didn't
apologize.
She made herself so small they would feel big.
She's gone—
I killed her before she ended us.

You think you found my weakness and can
destroy me—
Little did you know, I was my own
weakness.
I was an outsider in my own head.
I outcasted myself.
My mind was determined to drive me to madness.
I healed wounds that others and myself inflicted.
I conquered my mind and now it is my greatest
weapon.

Because nothing and no one illicits fear—
Only I did.
And I will never relinquish that control again.

I 'm not the one for you—
I won't coddle you.
I won't let you let your life pass you by.
I won't praise you for achieving the bare minimum.
I will push you to challenge yourself.
I will remind you that your dreams will not wait for
you for forever.
I will remind you that this is your one and only
chance.
I will encourage you to break as many glass ceilings
as possible.
But know this—
I will sit with you while you regain your strength.
I will help you heal.
I will train with you.
I will fight right alongside you.
I will celebrate your victories.
I will strategize with you.
I won't let you quit—
But I will help you win.

There is no growth without pain.
There is no triumph without sacrifice.
There is no knowledge without mistakes.
There is no gratitude without despair.
There is no life without death.

*What are you carrying? Put it down.*_____

_____

_____

_____

_____

_____

_____

_____

_____

_____

_____

_____

_____

_____

Share your thoughts with the_poetry_playlist

I Can't Live Like This

Meet You at the Graveyard
Cleffy

I can't live like this.
I was born to live;
To thrive—
Not merely survive.
I was born to feel
Every ounce of pain
That threatens to make me numb;
Each burst of joy
That leads me to tears.
I was born to run free—
Not to crawl on the ground
And always be near my grave.

I refuse to become them—
To live on my knees,
Never knowing how to stand on my own.
I refuse to live a life for others—
To move as their puppet,
Never knowing how to coordinate my own moves.
I refuse to be their soldier—
To live a life only following orders,
Never knowing how to become a warrior.
I refuse to repeat history—
To never learn the lesson,
Never knowing how to evolve from the past.

*T*he irony of it all;
   If you take away sorrow,
      You take away the memory.
If you take away betrayal,
You take away the ability to trust.
If you take away the scar,
You take away the healing.
If you take away the rejection,
You take away the opportunity.
If you take away the vulnerability,
You take away the authenticity.
If you take away the ending,
You take away the beginning.

*W*e assume a lot—
   We assume love is monogamous with joy;
      We assume pain is attached to something
we should let go;
We assume joy is accompanied with large numbers;
We assume silence is boredom;
We assume death is a thief.
We assume without expanding our knowledge.

*W*hat do I want my legacy to be?
   That I was brave—
      I looked in the abyss of uncertainty

And decided to jump anyways.
I was laughed at for dreaming too big—
Now they ask, in awe, how I brought my dreams to life.
They told me I was unrealistic—
All my desires continue to transpire.
They said I would only be useful for my looks—
Now my words bring them to their knees.
When I had everything to lose,
I chose to go all in on myself.

What do you want your legacy to be? _____

_____

_____

_____

_____

_____

_____

_____

_____

_____

_____

_____

_____

_____

Share your thoughts with the_poetry_playlist

How Cruel It Is

Experience
Ludovico Einaudi

*H*ow cruel it is,
To love only for it to be misplaced;
To have memories but have no one to
share them with;
To mourn someone whose heart still beats;
To lay youth to rest when they never got the chance
to experience being tired;
To never become well acquainted with oneself for
you always impersonated another;
To never heal a wound inflicted by another, only to
become the cause of its fatality;
To be frozen in time while the hourglass still
moved;
To volunteer to be on the front lines when it was
never your war;
To become a prisoner of your own mind when it
serves to liberate you.

*I*t's quite the paradox, isn't it?
The feeling of emptiness we carry—
It should be weightless,
Like carrying a feather.
Yet, it's the heaviest thing to be carried.
You have nothing but are burdened by everything.

*I*f a day comes where you feel unlovable,
Know that others still remember how your
laugh is highly infectious;
How your hugs give them more warmth than any
fire;
How your love makes them feel invincible.
Know that others will hear a song that reminds them
of you and they can't help but smile;
How your belief in them is more valuable than gold;
How you lent them a hand when they were
drowning, and now they watch sunsets in peace.
Know that they remember—
You just need to remember to give yourself grace.

*B*aby girl,
I warned you.
You didn't stand a chance.
When your eyes looked upon his beauty,
You became blind to your own.
When he spoke those beautiful lies,
You couldn't hear the truth.
When he touched you,
You lost touch with reality.
When you met him,
You lost yourself.

*H*ere's to them—
  To those who loved more than they were
  loved;
To those who are constantly someone's person,
But do not have a person for themselves;
To those who have been shunned for being
authentic,
By people who hide in the masses;
To those who gave unwavering support
Yet remained deserted.
The hour has come for those with a golden heart
And a bleeding soul—
Your time is now.

*W*hat you did wasn't what broke me.
  Yes, you lied to me, and betrayed me.
  You were the one person who convinced
me to hand over my heart—
That it was the safest place to be.
I didn't see it coming.
The biggest betrayal of it all
Is the inability to trust myself anymore.

*L*oving you feels like I am the mightiest ship,
Able to withstand any distance or storm.
You not loving me back,
Forever anchors my ship in the harbor.
I'll never outlast the most unforgiving storms and come out victorious.
I'll never feel the freedom of the wind guiding me
Taking me to where I yearn to be.
Instead, I will be shackled to the harbor—
Never to experience freedom and its endless possibilities,
And restrained to an ordinary life.

*How have you betrayed yourself?*_____

_____

_____

_____

_____

_____

_____

_____

_____

_____

_____

_____

_____

_____

_____

Share your thoughts with the_poetry_playlist

Few Know What It's Like to Live in the Fog

Je Te Laisserai Des Mots
Patrick Watson

*F*ew know what it's like to live in the fog
and emerge back into the light.
You initially entered the beautiful forest—
You know it is beautiful, and you should be
absorbed in awe and astonishment.
Yet,
The sun fades, and fog creeps up on you,
demanding your full attention.
The forest is now blanketed in a dense fog.
You can only see one step at a time.

Panic begins to race through your veins faster and
faster.
You stumble, trying to find your way out,
But end up going in circles.
Before long, all you can do is lay down and hope
that the fog lifts or that someone finds you.
But no one knows your mind dictated your
journey—
You have been mentally removed.
In return, your physical distance goes unnoticed.
Before you know it, too much time has passed.
You are not the same person that entered this once
beautiful forest—
You can't remember life before the fog.
The fog rendered everything dull—
You can't even see the brilliant green of the foliage.

The fog brought the chill that made you feel
numb—
Your memories lost their vibrancy.
You can't recall how the sun felt on your face.
You are completely isolated, not only from the rest
of the world, but from yourself.
Then a voice whispers,
"One step at a time is all you need."

So, you separate yourself from lying on the frigid
forest floor, for this is not the day you become one.
You steady your breath.
You take one step at a time.
You stumble, but it reaffirms you are trying to get
out.
Before you know it, the fog is slowly withdrawing.
You feel it proceeding away from you and your
mind.
You can see and think more clearly.
Every now and then the fog threatens to take hold of
you again—
However, you breathe and take one step at a time.

You start to hear voices in the distance—
You're not sure if it is a memory or if it is real.
You begin to feel the sun on your face.
It embraces you in its warmth.

It's something you never expected to experience again.
And with that last step,
You find yourself in a clearing.
You observe people laughing and embracing each other, absolutely unfazed by your presence.
They have no idea the journey you have just returned from—
One where you saved yourself.
You leave the forest behind and vow to never forget—
"One step at a time".

*One step at a time*_____

_____

_____

_____

_____

_____

_____

_____

_____

_____

_____

_____

_____

_____

_____

Share your thoughts with the_poetry_playlist

Meet the Author

Aurora Burkhart has always embraced her entrepreneurial spirit and vivid imagination. As a child, she was naturally curious, exploring ideas and cultivating creativity. In adulthood, she transformed her interests into tangible skills, eventually inventing her own product and running her own business.

Rather than labeling herself as an "inventor" or "entrepreneur," Aurora sees herself as a creative thinker dedicated to using her imagination to support others in meaningful ways. One of her favorite creative outlets is poetry.

Aurora rediscovered her love for writing poems during a pivotal moment in her life. With music as her muse, she began crafting heartfelt pieces that helped her stay grounded while letting her thoughts flow freely. This powerful connection between music and words inspired The Poetry Playlist, a project that brings together her passion for creativity and her desire to inspire others.